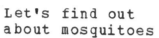

LET'S FIND
OUT ABOUT

mosquitoes

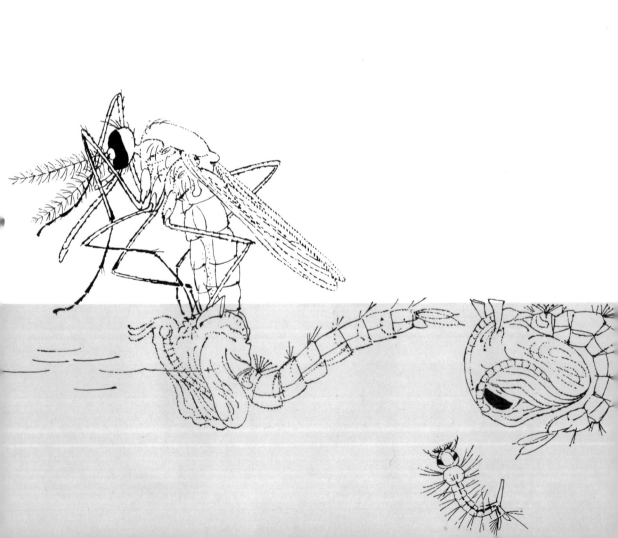

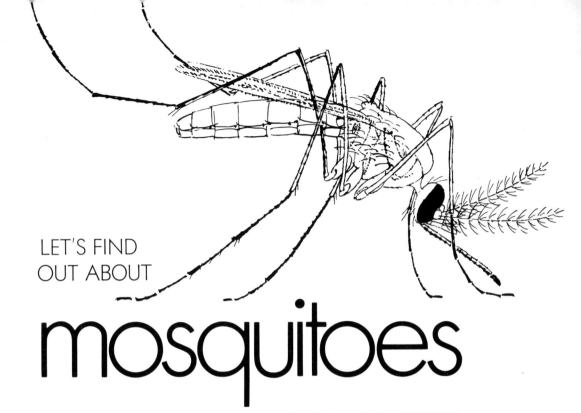

LET'S FIND
OUT ABOUT

mosquitoes

BY DAVID WEBSTER

illustrated by Arabelle Wheatley

FRANKLIN WATTS | NEW YORK | LONDON

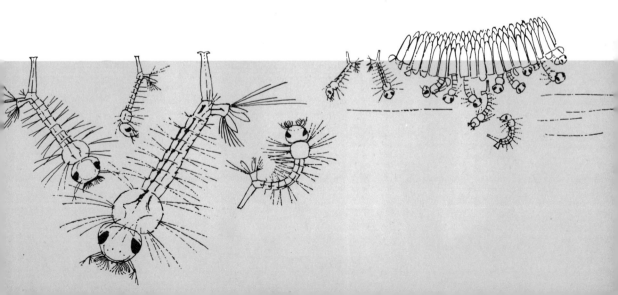

Library of Congress Cataloging in Publication Data

Webster, David, 1930-
       Let's find out about mosquitoes.

       SUMMARY: Introduces the physical characteristics and
habits of the mosquito.
       1. Mosquitoes — Juvenile literature. |1. Mosquitoes|
I. Wheatley, Arabelle, illus. II. Title.
QL536.W43   595.7'71   74-4154
ISBN 0-531-02740-6

Nobody likes mosquitoes. A mosquito bite
hurts. You have probably been bitten by
mosquitoes many times.

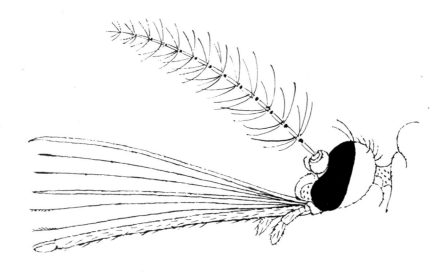

Do you know how a mosquito bites? It has a
long beak which is called a *proboscis*.
The beak is made of several different parts.
Inside a covering are four sharp bristles and
two thin tubes. The bristles jab up and down
to make a hole in your thick skin. Soon the cut
begins to bleed. The mosquito sucks your blood
up in one tube. It spits saliva out the other tube.
The saliva may help keep the blood from
clotting; it also makes the bite itch.

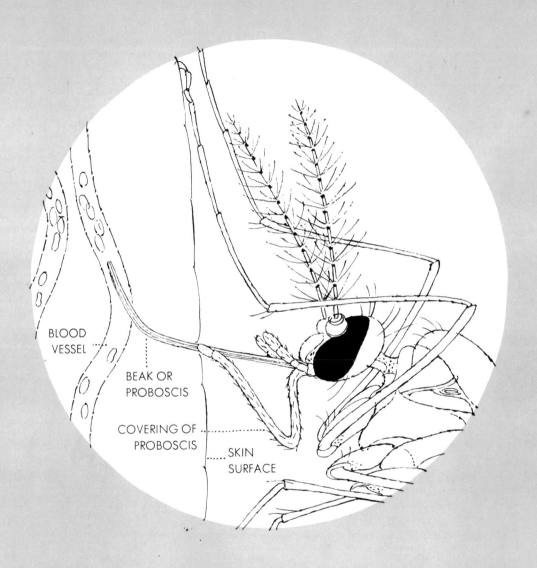

BLOOD
VESSEL

BEAK OR
PROBOSCIS

COVERING OF
PROBOSCIS

SKIN
SURFACE

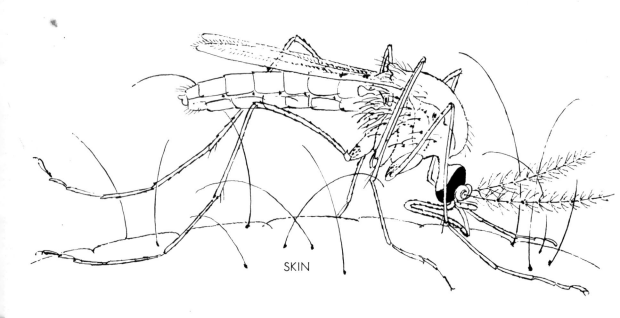

SKIN

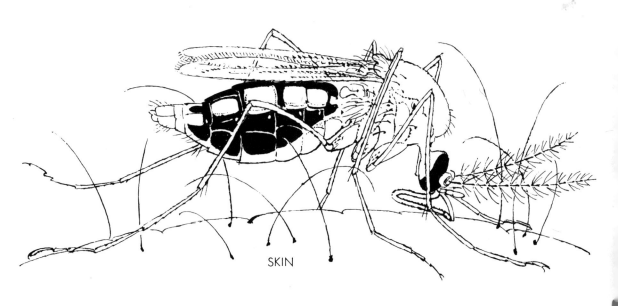

SKIN

The mosquito will suck blood for several
minutes—unless you swat it first. Its body
swells up like a balloon. The mosquito can still
fly with its big load of blood. Now the mosquito
can rest for several days, for it takes that long
for the blood meal to be digested.

9

Not all mosquitoes are alike. There are many different kinds of mosquitoes. You have probably been bitten by one of the three kinds of mosquitoes shown here. Although the many different kinds of mosquitoes look alike, each has different habits of living and mating.

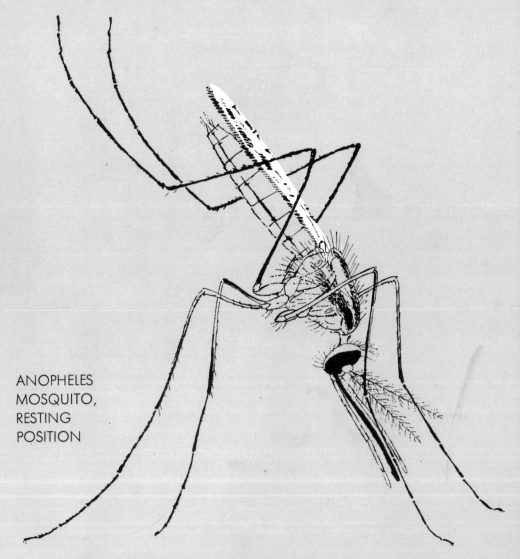

ANOPHELES
MOSQUITO,
RESTING
POSITION

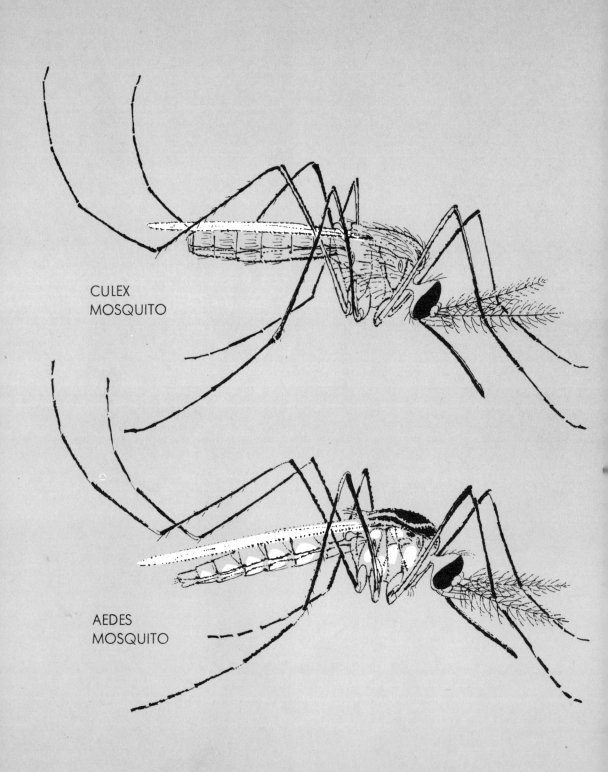

CULEX
MOSQUITO

AEDES
MOSQUITO

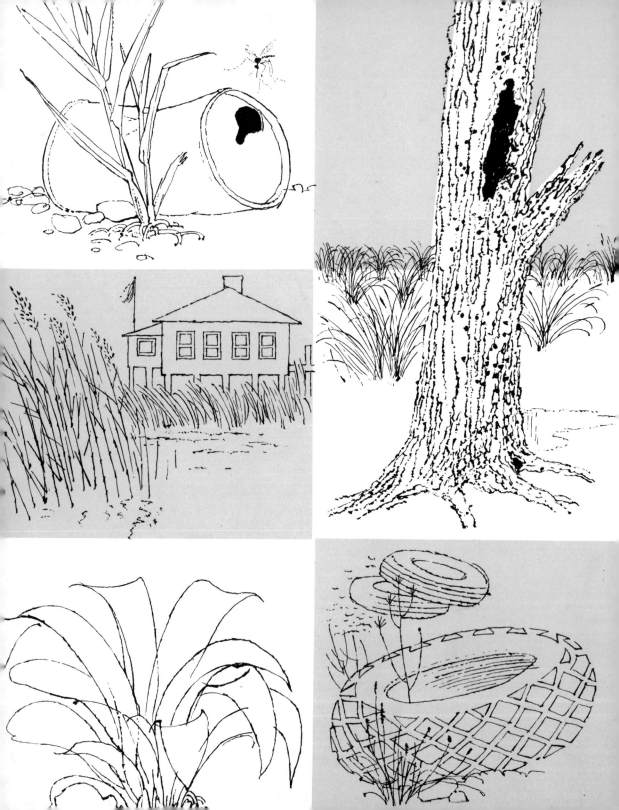

During the winter, mosquitoes do not seem to be anywhere in sight. Later, in the spring, mosquitoes can be found almost anywhere. Did you ever think about where all of the mosquitoes come from?

Mosquitoes grow from eggs.

Certain kinds of female mosquitoes who are going to lay eggs sleep during the winter. Their male mates die when winter comes.

When the female wakes up in the spring, she lays eggs in a wet place. She might use rain water in an old tire or tin can. Or she could find a quiet place in a swamp or mud puddle.

Other kinds of female mosquitoes lay eggs in the summer. The female is so light she can stand on the water. She drops her eggs one at a time. The eggs are very sticky. The female sticks the eggs together with her hind feet. Finally there are hundreds of eggs in the tiny raft.

When winter comes, all of the male and female mosquitoes die. The eggs live through the winter to become mosquitoes the following year.

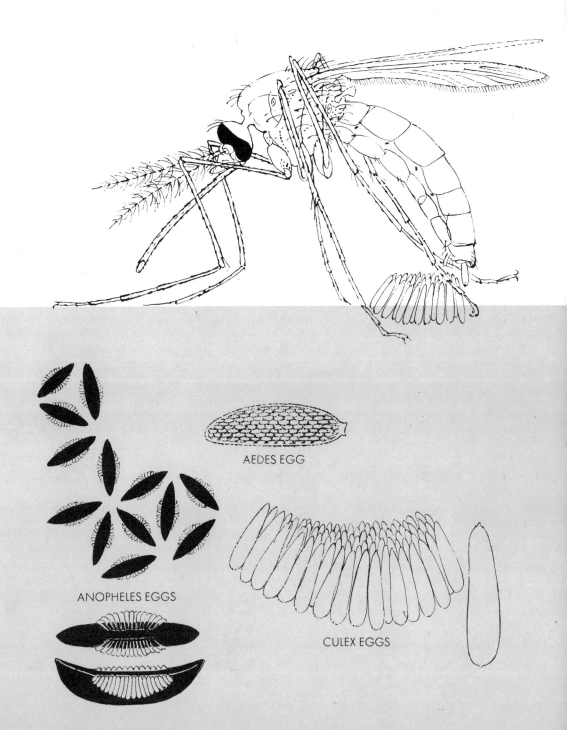

AEDES EGG

ANOPHELES EGGS

CULEX EGGS

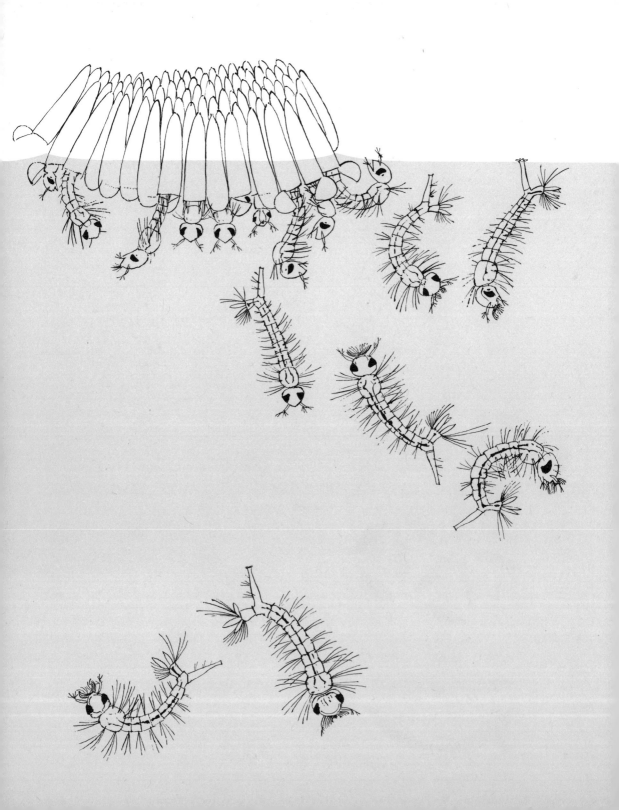

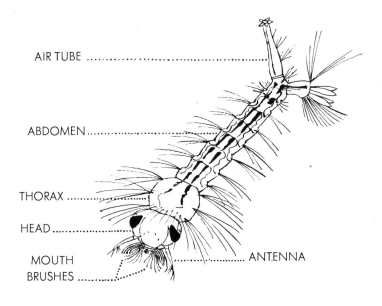

AIR TUBE ....

ABDOMEN...

THORAX ....

HEAD..................................

MOUTH
BRUSHES ....

ANTENNA

What do you think hatches from a mosquito egg? It is *not* a mosquito. It is a tiny mosquito wiggler. It does not look anything like a grown-up mosquito. It lives in the water. Much of its time is spent hanging at the surface. Here the wiggler breathes air through its air tube. When scared, the wiggler wiggles to the bottom for protection.

Many mosquito wigglers do not live long. They are eaten by other animals. Fish, tadpoles, turtles, and ducks eat many wigglers. Sometimes wigglers even eat each other.

As the wiggler eats and grows, it must shed its
skin. The skin cannot grow larger. So the dead
skin splits off and floats away.

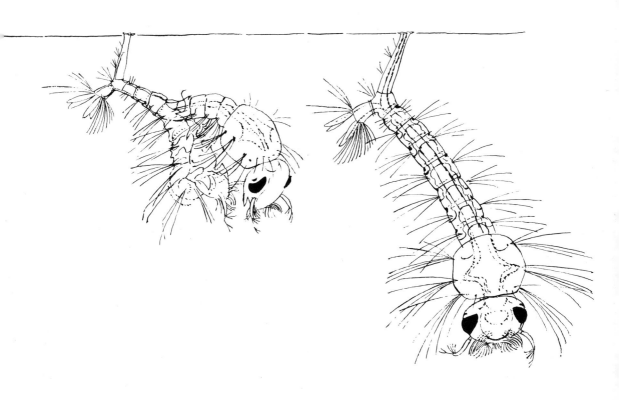

Can you guess why you do not shed your skin
as you grow?

21

The wiggler is about a half-inch long after it has shed three times. Something strange happens the next time the wiggler sheds its skin. The new wiggler looks much different. It is darker and shaped like a comma. Now it is called a *pupa*.

The pupa does not eat. It usually floats quietly on the surface. The pupa breathes through two tubes at its front end.

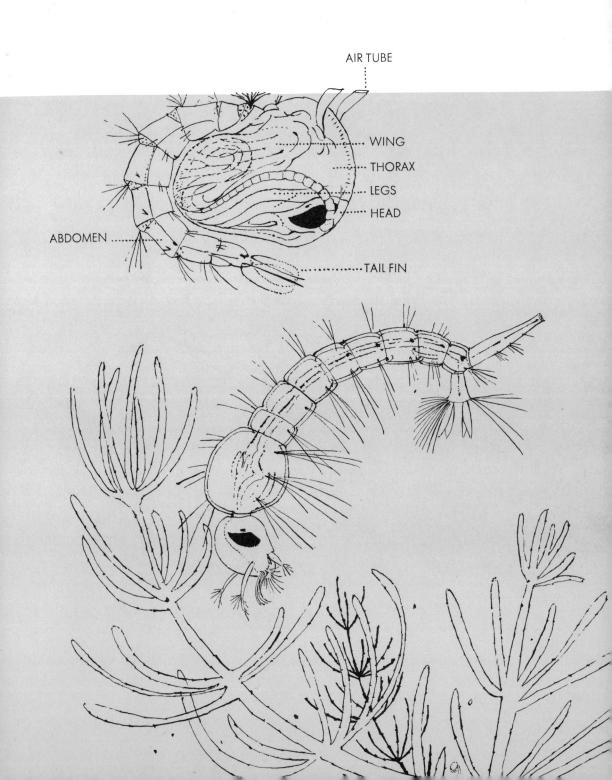

AIR TUBE

WING

THORAX

LEGS

HEAD

ABDOMEN

TAIL FIN

Big things happen inside the pupa. Legs and wings begin to form. In a few days the pupa pumps air into its stomach. The fat stomach makes the pupa's skin split open along the back. And out steps a mosquito.

The mosquito cannot fly until its wings have hardened. It rests on the water for about an hour. Then the mosquito flies away. The little egg has finally become an adult mosquito.

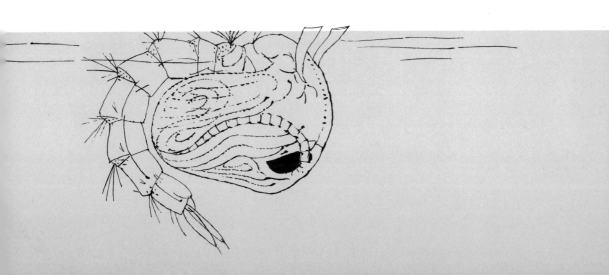

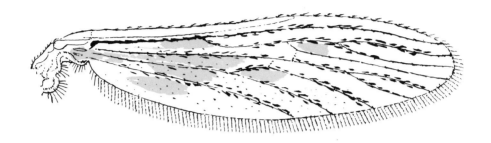

The wings of a mosquito look very frail. But with them a mosquito can fly quite fast. At top speed it goes about 30 miles per hour. However, it does not fly very high. This is why no screens are needed in the upper windows of tall buildings.

A mosquito makes a buzzing sound as it flies near your ear. Where does this noise come from? It is made by the flapping of the mosquito's wings. The wings go up and down more than 300 times each second. That is much too fast for us to see.

Usually a mosquito flies around only at night. The heat from the sun would dry out the insect and might kill it. Where could a mosquito hide during the day?

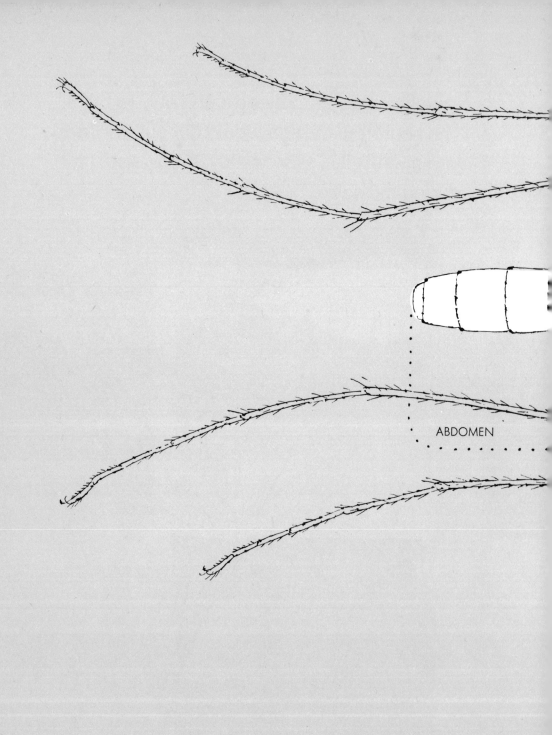

ABDOMEN

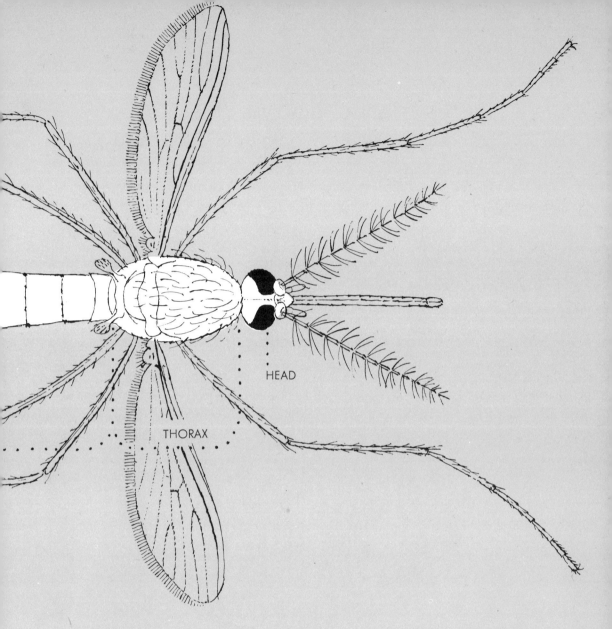

HEAD

THORAX

Like all insects, a mosquito has three parts to its body. There is a head, a thorax, and an abdomen.

The head has two large eyes. There is also a pair of long feelers or antennae. These help a mosquito hear.

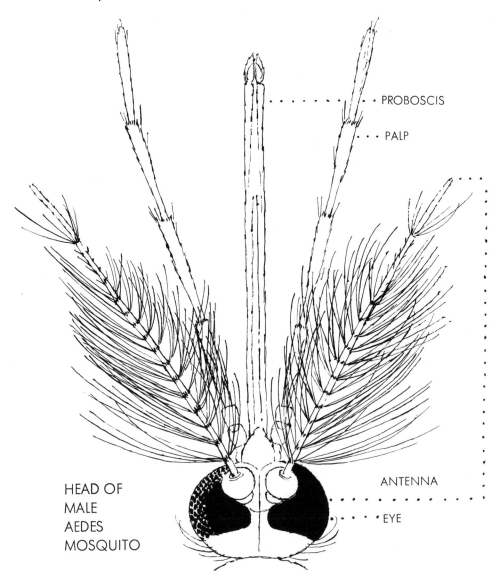

PROBOSCIS

PALP

ANTENNA

EYE

HEAD OF
MALE
AEDES
MOSQUITO

A male mosquito has bushy feelers. The antennae
of a female have fewer hairs. This is a good
way to tell a male mosquito from a female.

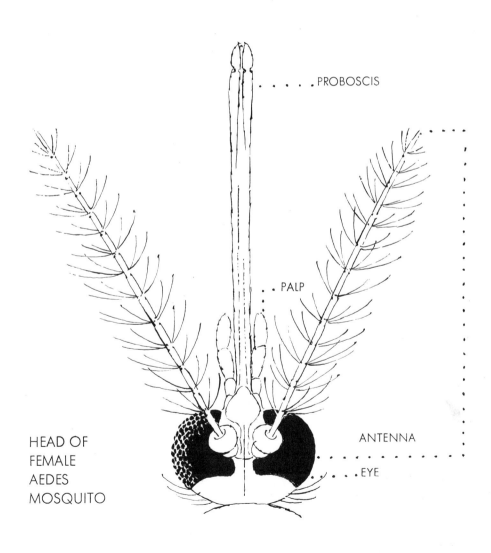

PROBOSCIS

PALP

ANTENNA

EYE

HEAD OF
FEMALE
AEDES
MOSQUITO

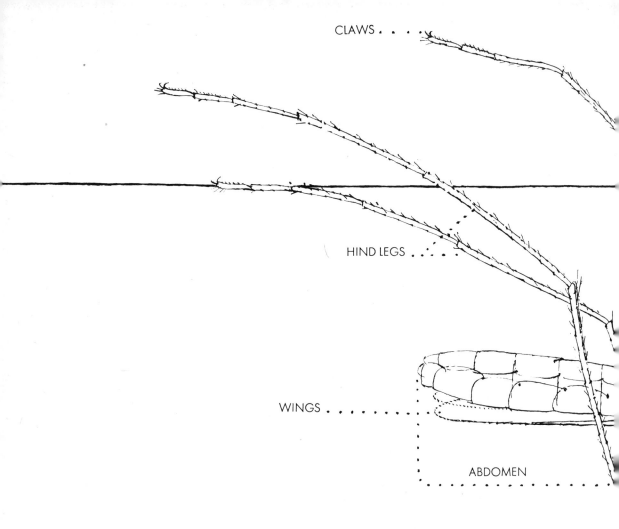

CLAWS . . . .

HIND LEGS . . .

WINGS . . . .

ABDOMEN

A mosquito has six skinny legs. All of them are
attached to the thorax. Each leg has a tiny claw
instead of a foot. The mosquito uses its claws
to hold on. Have you ever seen a mosquito
standing on the ceiling?

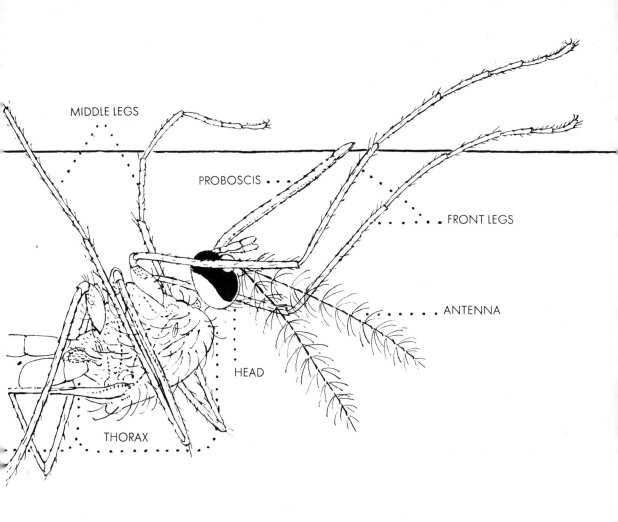

MIDDLE LEGS

PROBOSCIS

FRONT LEGS

ANTENNA

HEAD

THORAX

Female mosquitoes drink plant juices. Most of
them must also eat blood before they can lay
eggs that will hatch. Some kinds of female
mosquitoes feed on the blood of frogs. Another
kind prefers the blood of birds.

The mosquitoes you have probably seen suck
blood from larger animals, such as horses
and people.

A male mosquito cannot get blood because his mouth parts cannot cut into skin. No one has ever been bitten by a male mosquito. The male just drinks plant juices from flowers and leaves. He is seldom seen.

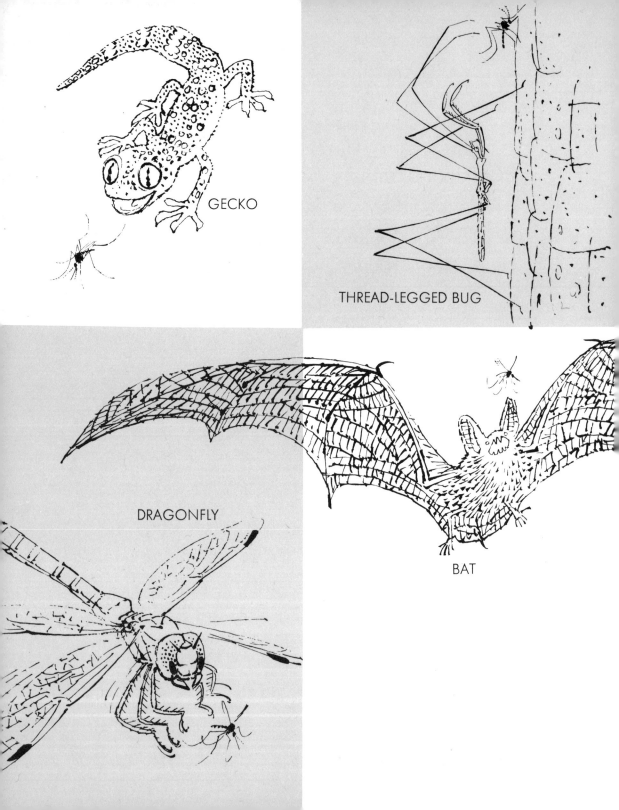

GECKO

THREAD-LEGGED BUG

DRAGONFLY

BAT

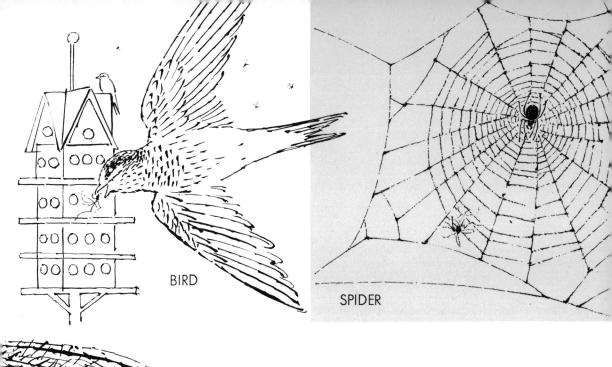

BIRD

SPIDER

Some kinds of mosquitoes die of old age in about a month. But many are killed by animals before that. A bat was found that had eaten 700 mosquitoes in one night. Other mosquitoes are eaten by dragonflies, birds, spiders, and frogs. Mosquitoes can also be killed by cold weather.

Some mosquitoes carry diseases that make humans sick. Many people in the jungle have been killed by malaria. To cause malaria, a mosquito must first bite someone who is sick. Then the mosquito bites a healthy person. The saliva of the mosquito contains malaria germs. The germs get into the healthy person's blood through the mosquito bite hole. Now this person is infected with malaria.

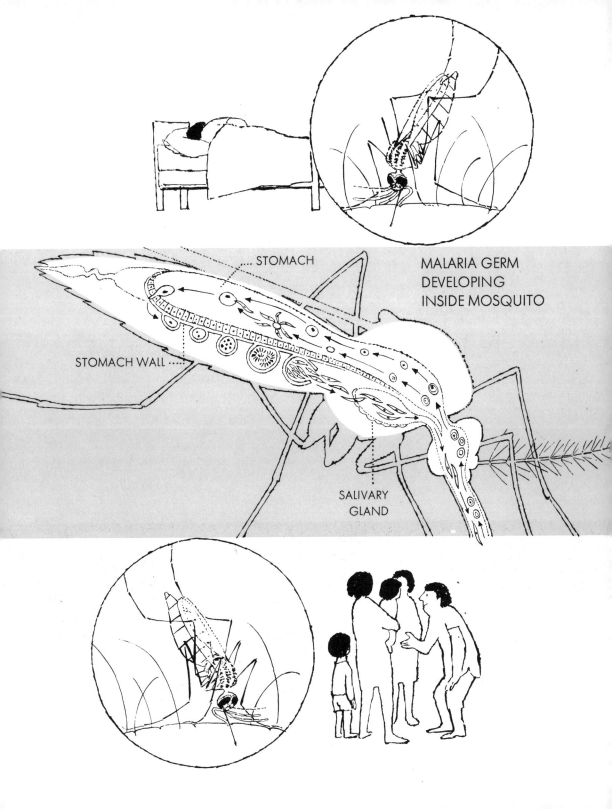

STOMACH

MALARIA GERM
DEVELOPING
INSIDE MOSQUITO

STOMACH WALL

SALIVARY
GLAND

Wigglers can be killed by spreading oil on swamps. The oil floats on top of the water and the wigglers cannot get through the oil to breathe the air. Sometimes fish are put into swamps to eat the wigglers. Swamps can also be drained so there is no water for the wigglers to live in.

Adult mosquitoes are killed by poison sprays. Sometimes airplanes spray poison on swamps where mosquitoes live.

But other animals can also be hurt when mosquitoes are sprayed. Many birds must eat mosquitoes and other insects. Without insects the birds will die.

Some birds get sick when eating insects that have been sprayed with poison.

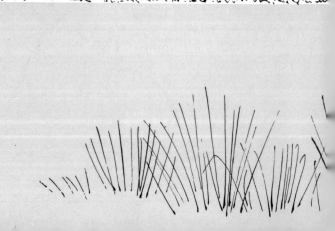

Men kill mosquitoes because they carry disease. Mosquitoes are also annoying to people who want to be outside.

Men kill mosquitoes because they don't like them. But birds and other animals like lots of mosquitoes. Without this kind of food, some animals cannot live.

Are mosquitoes good or bad?

ABOUT THE AUTHOR

David Webster is a former elementary and junior high school science teacher and served for four years as director of science for the Lincoln, Massachusetts school system. He is now a consultant for the Wellesley public schools, and has written numerous science-activity articles for children's magazines.

Mr. Webster is the author of *Track Watching*, which was selected as an honor book by the New York Academy of Science. His other books published by Franklin Watts are *Photo Fun: A Manual for Shutterbugs* and *How to do a Science Project (A First Book)*.